PICTURE A COUNTRY

Egypt

Henry Pluckrose

W
FRANKLIN WATTS
LONDON • SYDNEY

This is the Egyptian flag.

First Published in 1998
by Franklin Watts
This edition 2001

Franklin Watts
96 Leonard Street
London EC2A 4XD

Franklin Watts Australia
56 O'Riordan Street
Alexandria, Sydney
NSW 2015

© Franklin Watts 1998

ISBN 0 7496 4290 4

A CIP catalogue record for this book is
available from the British Library

Dewey Decimal Classification Number: 916.2

10 9 8 7 6 5 4 3 2 1

Series Editor: Rachel Cooke
Designer: Kirstie Billingham
Picture research: Juliet Duff

Printed in Great Britain

Photographic acknowledgements:

Cover: Robert Harding Picture Library t, Eye Ubiquitous
cr (Paul Stewart), Getty Images cr (Werner Otto),
Travel Ink b (Abbie Enock).

AA Photo Library p. 16;
J. Allan Cash pp. 11t, 28;
Axiom Photographic Agency pp. 8 & 23 (James Morris),
13, 14, 19 & 24 (Alex Misiewicz);
James Davis Travel Photography p. 29t;
Eye Ubiquitous p. 21 (Paul Stewart);
Getty Images pp. 10 (Werner Otto), 18, 22b;
Robert Harding Picture Library pp. 9, 11b, 12, 15 (Nigel
Francis), 17, 22t, 26, 27;
Travel Ink pp. 25, 29 (Abbie Enock)
Chirstine Osborne Pictures pp. 20.

All other photography Steve Shott.
Map by Julian Baker.

Contents

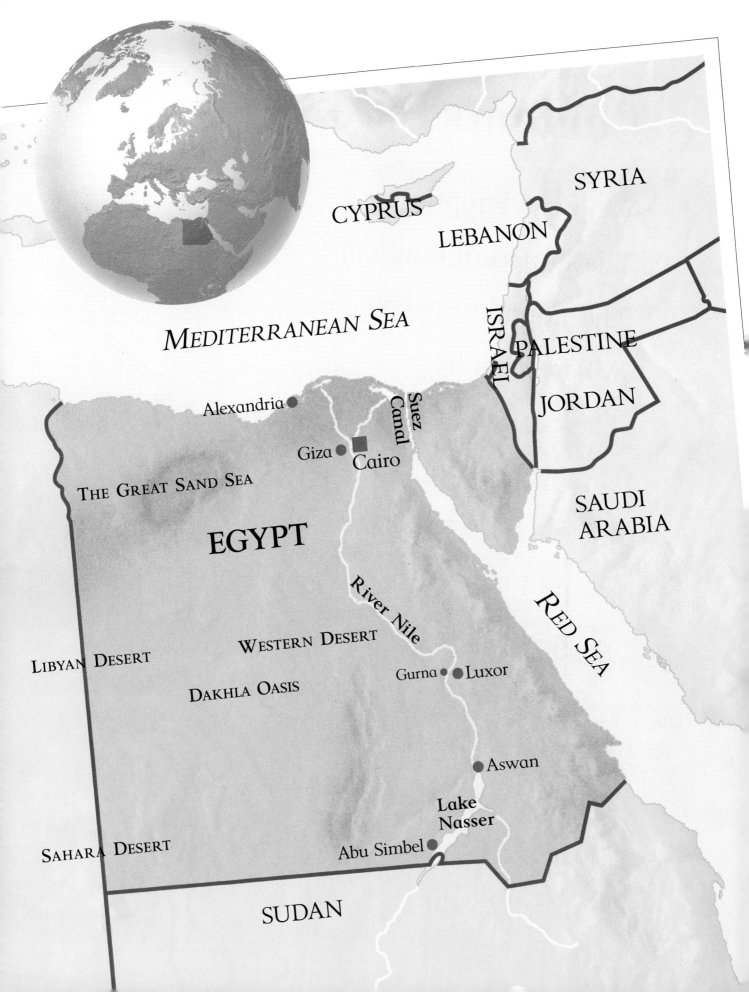

CYPRUS

SYRIA

LEBANON

ISRAEL

PALESTINE

JORDAN

MEDITERRANEAN SEA

Suez Canal

SAUDI
ARABIA

Alexandria

Giza
Cairo

THE GREAT SAND SEA

EGYPT

LIBYAN DESERT

WESTERN DESERT

DAKHLA OASIS

River Nile

RED SEA

Gurna • • Luxor

Aswan

Lake
Nasser

SAHARA DESERT

Abu Simbel

SUDAN

Where is Egypt?

This is a map of Egypt.
Egypt is a country in which
two continents meet.
Part of Egypt is in Africa,
part of Egypt is in Asia.

Here are some
Egyptian stamps
and money.

Egyptian money
is counted in pounds.

The Egyptian landscape

Egypt is a country of deserts.

A desert is a place where very little rain falls.

Deserts are usually very hot or very cold.

In Egypt, the deserts are hot

as the sun shines all day.

But, at night, they become a lot colder.

Deserts do not all look the same. This is part of
Egypt's Western Desert called the White Desert.

The Nile is the longest river in the world.
It is 6670 kilometres long. This is the Nile at Aswan.

The River Nile runs through Egypt.
It is very important, as it brings water
to the land along its banks.

This great temple at Abu Simbel was built over 3000 years ago, when the pharaoh Ramses II ruled Egypt.

The Egyptian people

People have lived in Egypt for thousands of years.
They lived along the River Nile and
built cities, villages, palaces and temples.

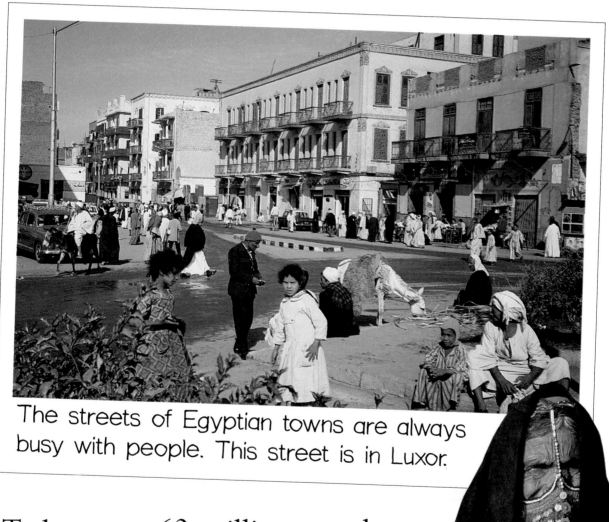

The streets of Egyptian towns are always
busy with people. This street is in Luxor.

Today over 60 million people
live in Egypt.
They speak and write Arabic.

Where they live

Most Egyptians live in towns and villages along the River Nile.

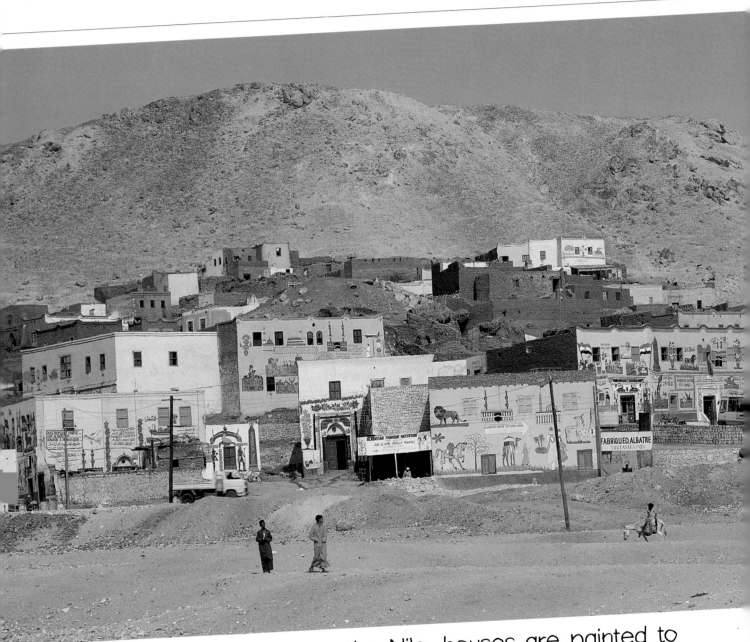

In the village of Gurna on the Nile, houses are painted to celebrate pilgrimages to Mecca, the Muslims' sacred city.

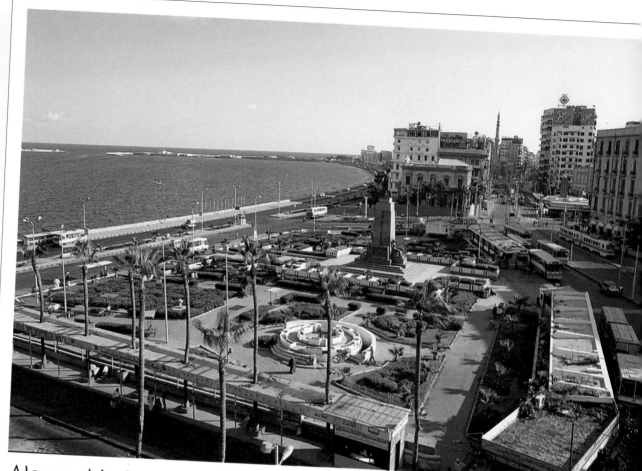

Alexandria is on the Mediterranean coast of Egypt. Today, it is a busy, modern city.

The city of Alexandria is Egypt's largest port. It was founded and named by Alexander the Great, the Greek king who conquered Egypt in 332 BC.

The capital city

Cairo is the capital of Egypt.
Over 16 million people live there.
It is an old city but there are
many new buildings alongside
the older ones.

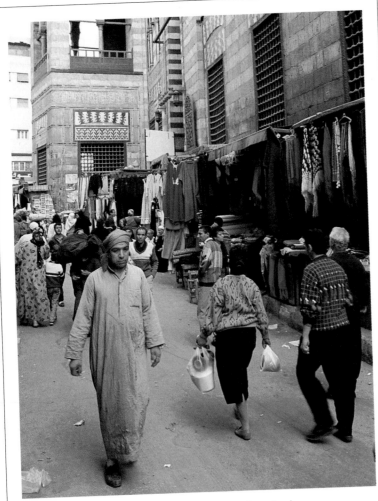

This is a clothes market in a
street in old Cairo.

Like most of Egypt's towns and cities, Cairo is built on the banks of the River Nile.

Canals and dams

The Suez Canal runs across Egypt. It joins the Mediterranean to the Red Sea and the Indian Ocean. It was built so that great ships could travel between Europe and Asia without going around Africa. Ships pay to use the canal.

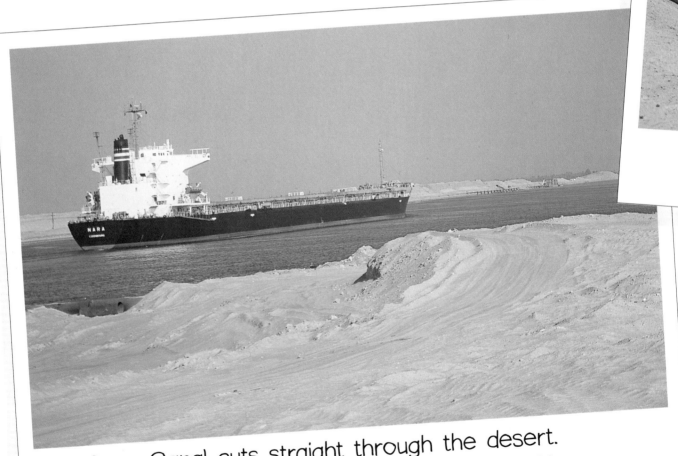

The Suez Canal cuts straight through the desert. It is 169 kilometres long and was opened in 1869.

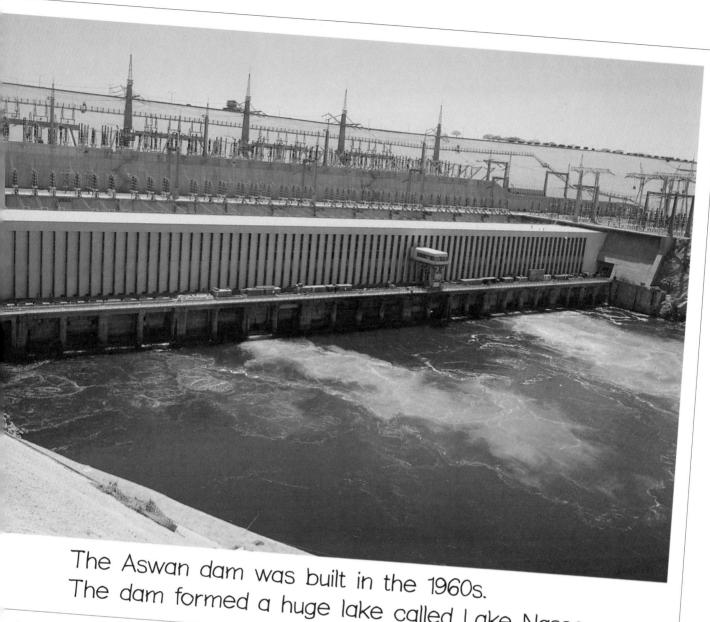

The Aswan dam was built in the 1960s.
The dam formed a huge lake called Lake Nasser.

An enormous dam has been built
across the Nile at Aswan.
It is used to make electricity.
The dam also controls how much water
flows down the river.

Farming

Egyptian farmers grow many
crops along the Nile valley.
They grow maize, rice, sugar cane, cotton,
fruit, vegetables, olives and grapes.
They keep goats, cattle, sheep and chickens.

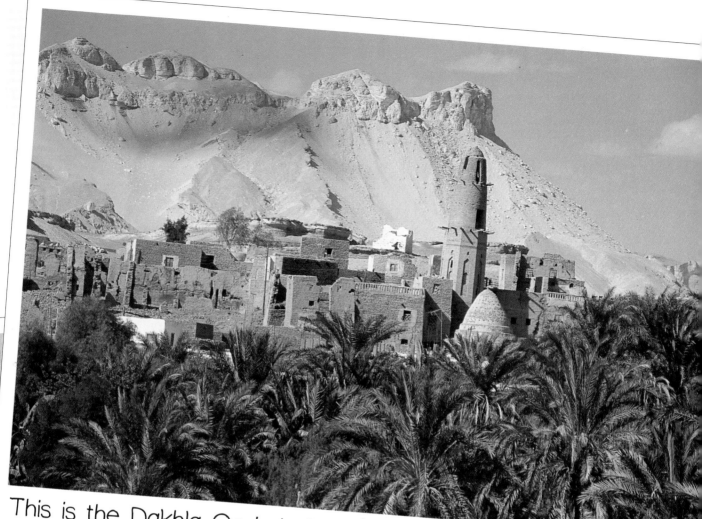

This is the Dakhla Oasis in Egypt's Western Desert. About 75,000 people live in this oasis region.

Farmers can also grow crops at oases in the desert.

An oasis (plural "oases") is a place in the desert where water bubbles up from under the ground.

19

Family life

Many Egyptian families
work on small farms.
Their homes are in country villages
or towns.

This Egyptian family is eating a meal. The mother covers her head, like many Egyptian women.

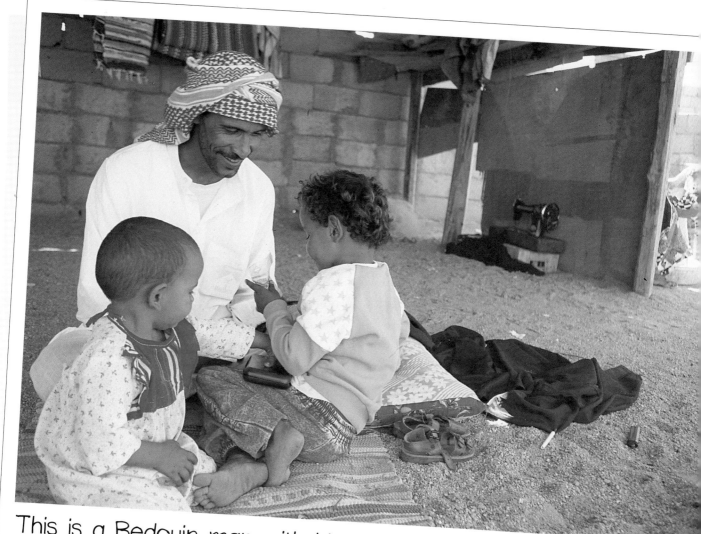

This is a Bedouin man with his children. Bedouin men often wear red and white cloths on their heads.

Some of the people of Egypt are nomads, who do not always live in one place. They are called Bedouins. They have a home which moves with them - a tent.

Egyptian food

Egyptians enjoy all kinds of different food. With every meal, they eat a sort of bread which is round and flat.

This is a dish of stuffed vine leaves.

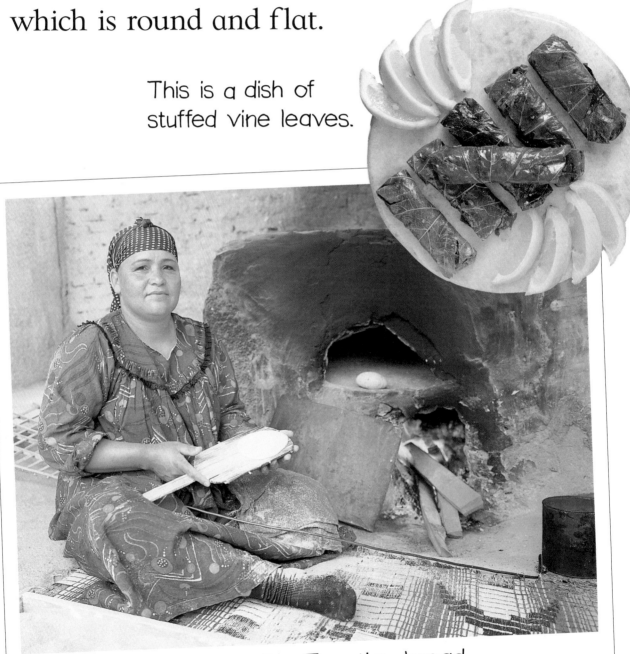

This woman is baking flat Egyptian bread.

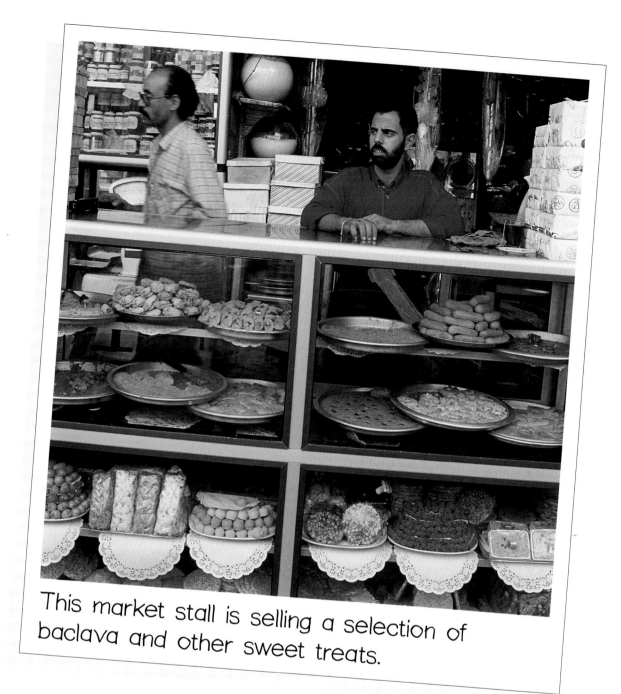

This market stall is selling a selection of baclava and other sweet treats.

Egyptians like kebabs, which are cubes of meat cooked on a stick. They enjoy fish, fried bean cakes called ta'maia, rice, goat's cheese and sweet pastries called baclava, which contain nuts and honey.

Out and about

Egyptians take part in water sports -
fishing, scuba diving, windsurfing and sailing.

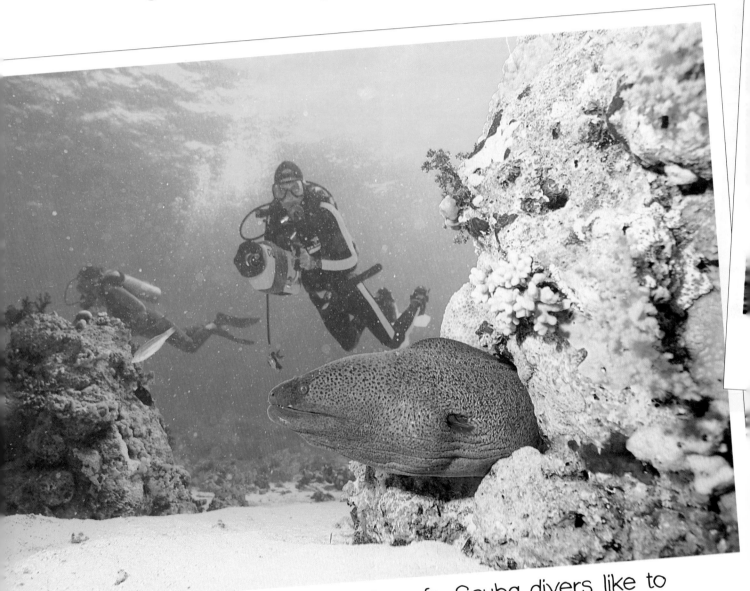

The Red Sea is full of coral reefs. Scuba divers like to explore the reefs as many colourful fish live there.

These posters are advertising Egyptian films.
The films are usually full of action and adventure.

They like to watch weight-lifting and
wrestling competitions.
People also go to see camel racing.
The cinema is very popular in Egypt and
a lot of films are made there each year.

Mosques and festivals

Egypt is an Islamic country.
This means that most Egyptians are Muslims
and follow the teachings of Mohammed.
Muslims go to the mosque to worship God.

People go to pray
at the Mohammed
Ali mosque in Cairo.

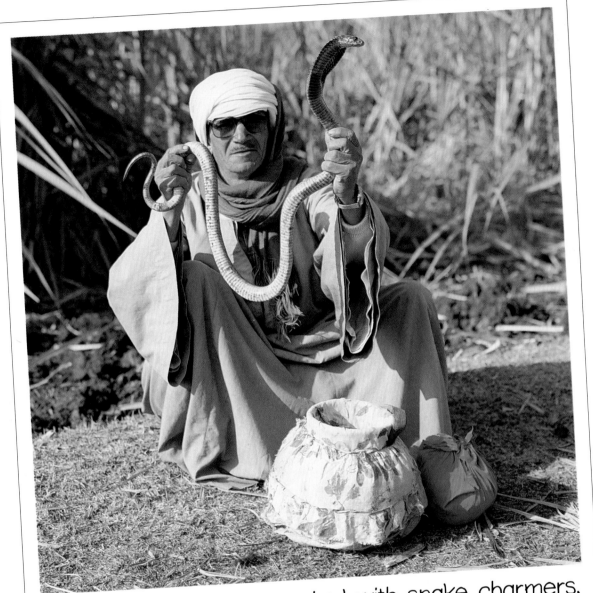

Mawlid is a religious carnival with snake charmers, prancing horses and dancers.

Each year, the Egyptians have religious festivals that often celebrate things to do with their daily lives, like fishing and horses.

Visiting Egypt

If you go to Egypt, you might go down the River Nile by boat to visit the temples and pyramids built by the ancient Egyptians.

The pyramids are tombs built for the pharaohs of ancient Egypt. This is the Great Pyramid at Giza.

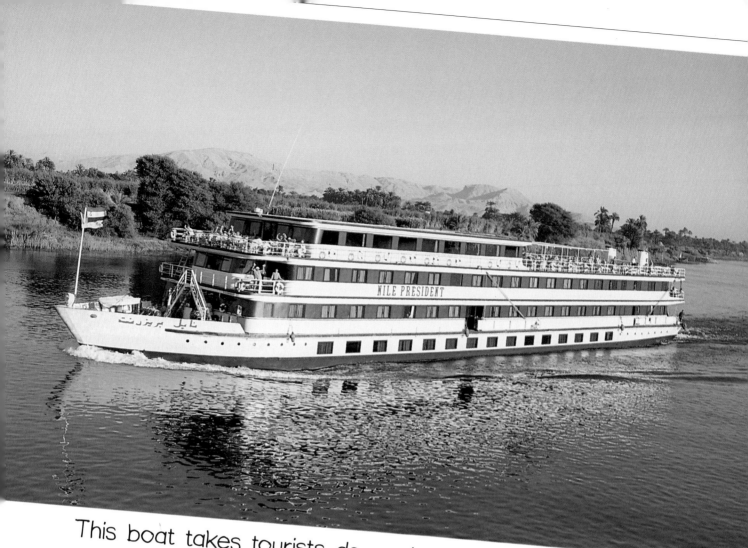

This boat takes tourists down the Nile. The boat is like a floating hotel. People eat and sleep on it.

You might explore a bazaar - a market where you can find bags, belts, pots, jewellery, rugs and blankets. You might even try to buy a camel!

Index

About this book

The last decade of the 20th century has been marked by an explosion in communications technology. The effect of this revolution upon the young child should not be underestimated. The television set brings a cascade of ever-changing images from around the world into the home, but the information presented is only on the screen for a few moments before the programme moves on to consider some other issue.

Instant pictures, instant information do not easily satisfy young children's emotional and intellectual needs. Young children take time to assimilate knowledge, to relate what they already know to ideas and information which are new.

The books in this series seek to provide snapshots of everyday life in countries in different parts of the world. The images have been selected to encourage the young reader to look, to question, to talk. Unlike the TV picture, each page can be studied for as long as is necessary and subsequently returned to as a point of reference. For example, forms of Egyptian dress might be compared with their own; a discussion might develop about the ways in which food is prepared and eaten in a country whose culture and customs are different from their own.

The comparison of similarity and difference is the recurring theme in each of the titles in this series. People in different lands are superficially different. Where they live (the climate and terrain) obviously shapes the sort of houses that are built, but people across the world need shelter; coins may look different, but in each country people use money.

At a time when the world seems to be shrinking, it is important for children to be given the opportunity to focus upon those things which are common to all the peoples of the world. By exploring the themes touched upon in the book, children will begin to appreciate that there are strands in the everyday life of human beings which are universal.